Learning To Walk By Faith Not By Sight

Problems and Answers for Everyday Situations

TRACY KINGSBURY

WESTBOW
PRESS
A DIVISION OF THOMAS NELSON

WestBow Press books may be ordered through booksellers or by contacting:

WestBow Press
A Division of Thomas Nelson
1663 Liberty Drive
Bloomington, IN 47403
www.westbowpress.com
1-(866) 928-1240

ISBN: 978-1-4497-3515-9 (sc)
ISBN: 978-1-4497-3514-2 (e)

Library of Congress Control Number: 2011963000

Printed in the United States of America

WestBow Press rev. date: 1/09/2012

Contents

Dedication

To my Lord and Savior Jesus Christ, who inspired me to write this book: I'm so thankful that You were always there for me. Your steadfastness has been just as Your Word promises in Hebrews 13:5, "I will never leave you nor forsake you" (NKJV).

Jesus, You're the best thing that ever happened to me. I've had my share of life's ups and downs, and if anyone should ever write my life story, You would be there between each line of pain and glory. There have been hard times, but for every moment I spent hurting there was a moment You spent just loving me.

I love you Jesus!

Acknowledgments

To my wonderful sons, Austin and Alex Sigourney, I'm so proud of you guys. Thank you for all your encouragement and support and for bearing with me. Thank you for not complaining about what we couldn't afford during the tough years. You guys are the best.

To my godly husband, Todd, and my three beautiful Christian stepdaughters, Kayla, Kandace, and Kareena Kingsbury, you're all a blessing from the Lord.

To my loving parents, Ken and Jan Powell, thank you for everything you've done for me over the years.

To my awesome brothers, Bob, Mike, and Jeff Powell, thank you for your willingness to always lend a helping hand.

To Emily Boka and Dennis and Jacque Rouse, thank you for all your prayers, enthusiasm, and help with finding a publisher for this book.

To my close friends, thank you so much for always being there for me. You girls are truly gifts from God.

To Carmen Bright, my cousin, you're like the sister I don't have. We've shared some amazing times together over the years.

To all my other awesome cousins, aunts, and family members, thank you for all love and kindness.

To everyone mentioned above, I'm so thankful that God has blessed my life with all of you. You are all so loving, caring, helpful, and amazing. I love you all!

To WestBow Press, thanks for all your encouragement and support.

Introduction

God has the answer for every situation we face. There is no problem that is too difficult for Him. He can make a way where there seems to be no way, no matter how bad things appear. When the world says it can't be done, God says it can! Believe that all things are possible with Him.

Most of us only call on God when we're in a desperate situation, and our backs are against the wall. Wouldn't our lives be so much easier if we'd turn to the Lord first instead of last? We tend to call upon our friends and family first for advice and help, and when none of that works, we finally decide to call upon God.

God has a master plan for our lives. The Bible tells us in Jeremiah 29:11-13, "For, I know the thoughts that I think toward you says the Lord, thoughts of peace and not of evil, to give you a future and hope. Then you will call upon me and go and pray to Me, and I will listen to you. And you will seek Me and find Me, when you search for Me with all your heart." (NKJV)

He only wants the best for us. Sometimes, in order for Him to prepare us, we have to go through a series of events that are difficult and extremely painful. What the Enemy meant for harm, God can work out for our good. Weeping may endure for a night, but joy comes in the morning. We can't always understand at the time why certain things are happening to us, but God has everything under control if we put our trust in Him.

I pray as you read these true stories of how God taught me to walk by faith and not by sight that you draw encouragement and hope for whatever trials you may be facing. God can move mountains on your behalf if you'll just put your faith in Him.

Don't be afraid to let go and let God be in control. He is an awesome God!

Chapter 1

It's Not Over until God Says It's Over

It was 1998, and God began to teach me my first big lesson in walking by faith, not by sight. My husband (who is now my ex-husband) wanted to try and refinance our house so we could get out from under some of the debt we had accumulated. At the time, interest rates were high, and I wasn't crazy about the idea of such a high rate. So, I just kept praying and asking God to let His will be done in the situation. One month later, the bank told us that our credit still wasn't very good. So I thought, *Okay, Lord, You know what's best for us. I know You see all the bills we have and how at any moment we could fall through the thin ice we are skating on.* We were having such a difficult time paying the payments every month.

Well, over the course of the next several months, we tried a couple more times to refinance, and the banks kept saying no. At first I was really disappointed, and then I remembered God works in seasons and when He closes one door, it's because He has a better plan in mind for us. We don't always understand, but we have to learn to trust that God will lead us in the right direction if we obey Him.

Getting a Brand-New House

A month later, God showed me why He had closed that door. He wanted to give me a brand-new house. If we had refinanced our home back in November of 1998, all the equity would have been used up, leaving us short on the down payment we needed for a brand-new house.

In December of 1998, my brother told me about some land that was for sale about a quarter of a mile from our parents' house. My heart's desire had always been to get a piece of land and build a home. Also, our son was about to start school, and we needed my mom to get him on and off the bus. So, without a moment's hesitation, my mouth opened, and the Holy Spirit had me say, "Let's each try to get a piece of that land next to each other." Then, I thought, *That's just downright funny. My credit stinks, and I don't even have one dollar saved in the bank.* I thought, *Lord, I couldn't even get the bank to refinance the house I currently own. How in the world can I have a new home?*

Then, my brother went on to tell me that there was just one problem. Somebody else had first dibs on the property. Still, I really felt the Holy Spirit was telling me that it was time for the desires of my heart to be fulfilled.

Thirty Days Passed

About thirty days passed, and we still hadn't heard anything on the land. My bills were still way out of control. I decided one day that I would default on my pension loan. This would help ease some of our financial pressure, but I wouldn't be able to take out another loan for one year as a result. I started praying and asking God what I should do about this.

The next day at work, I went upstairs to the finance department to get the forms I needed to default on my pension loan. When I came back to my desk, there was a message on my phone from my brother. He was telling me about another piece of property that became available just down the way from the land we wanted. One acre was selling for seventeen thousand dollars. The only problem was that the owners wanted five thousand dollars down, and my brother didn't have the money. I began to pray and ask God if He wanted me to help my brother. I called my finance department and asked them how much more money I could borrow from my pension, and they told me five thousand dollars.

I knew then that God had a plan and that when He tells you something, He will see it through to the end. I called my brother back and told him that I would lend him the money. He said, "Sis, I don't know when I can pay you back, but I can make the monthly payment." Then he asked, "What if the land you want becomes available before I can pay you back in full? What are you going to do?" I told him not to worry and that God would make a way for me.

A few weeks later, my brother walked up to me and handed me five thousand dollars. I was shocked. He told me that he received a huge tax refund, and he did some side jobs to earn the rest. Well, praise God! Right after that happened, I received a phone call telling me that the land I wanted had just become available. The other buyer couldn't get financed. There was just one problem: I was nine thousand dollars short. The land was selling for fourteen thousand dollars.

Dealing with the Bank

I went to the bank and tried to get a loan, and the loan officer told me that she would get back to me. Well, it was Friday, and by 4:30 p.m. I couldn't stand the suspense any longer, so I called her back.

She said, "Oh, I'm really sorry, but the guy that makes the decision on these loans has left for the weekend, so I'll have to call you back Monday."

I'm thinking to myself, "You've got to be kidding me. You think you're going to keep me wondering all weekend? Oh no, that's just not going work." So after we hung up, I started praying and asking God to have the bank call me back in the next fifteen minutes, before I had to leave to pick up my son, if it was really His will for me to have this land. Well, fifteen minutes passed, and still no phone call. I locked up the house and was headed to my car when I remembered that I had forgotten to give water to the dog. When I went to get the water, I heard the phone ringing. I nearly killed myself trying to get to the phone.

The woman from the bank was calling me back, and she said the weirdest thing had happened. She explained, "After we hung up, the boss returned, and I asked him about your loan. He said that they would probably approve it."

I was so excited that I just kept thanking God for being so good to me.

Monday morning came, and I got a phone call from the bank telling me, "Sorry, Tracy, but we just can't approve your loan."

I thought, *What? You're joking, right? Now what am I going to do?* Once again I prayed and asked God to help me out. You know, His timing is always right. Ten minutes later, my phone rang, and it was the owner of the property.

He said, "You know, I've been thinking. Instead of hassling with the bank, why don't you just make monthly payments to me until you sell your house?"

Praise God, the Lord had just saved me from paying a bunch of bank fees.

Isn't that just like God to always be working behind the scenes in the spiritual realm on our behalf? To paraphrase the saying, when God shuts a door, He always opens a better one, but we must get to the place in our lives where we have complete and total trust in Him. I thought, *God, You're amazing. What a faithful God I serve.* But wait, there's more. This story keeps taking so many twists and turns.

Selling My House

Now, I had the land, but I needed to get my house sold so that we could start building our new home. For forty days, I fasted until lunchtime. I really needed a miracle. Our home was an older one with only about 846 square feet and no basement. When we bought it in 1993, we got a good deal on it. We paid about forty-eight thousand dollars, but let me tell you, this house needed a complete overhaul on the inside. So we did just that, shortly after we moved in.

The kitchen was so disgusting that I could see under the house when I opened the bottom cupboards. I was afraid to even put any dishes in there.

I'll never forget one night when I opened a drawer to get out a dishtowel. Out jumped a mouse. I started screaming and running. You would have thought an ax murderer was chasing me. I was screaming so loud and my heart was racing so fast that I wasn't sure who was going to drop dead of a heart attack first, the mouse or me. My husband was out of town, so I went out and bought some traps. However, one of the traps was the kind where the mice just get stuck in the trap and don't die. I didn't know that until about 11:00 that night when I kept hearing a strange noise. I thought, "There is no way I can go off to bed knowing this mouse could possibly get away and come into my room." So I called my friend, and her boyfriend came and took the mouse away. After that incident, I had my husband start remodeling the kitchen. He had already finished gutting the rest of the house and had redone every room for me.

After my forty-day fast was up, I felt God was telling me that now was the time to touch up the house and get it ready to be sold. For a week straight, I went to work and then came home and worked until late in the evening, getting the house ready to put on the market. I told my husband that I really felt God wanted us to be ready by that Saturday to start letting people come to see it. We were selling it without a realtor because we desperately needed every penny that we would make off it.

My husband kept saying, "We'll never be ready by Saturday."

However, I knew in my heart that all things were possible with God.

On Friday night, we stayed up until 3:45 a.m. working on the house. Then we slept for three hours, got back up, and worked right up until noon on Saturday. Then we posted a sign out front and prayed that God would send us a buyer. We showed the house for three hours on Saturday and three hours on Sunday. Several people came through, but nobody offered a purchase agreement. By 5:00 p.m. on Sunday, I prayed and asked God to send me a buyer with money so that I wouldn't have to show the house again the next weekend

Well, by 7:00 p.m. that night, I received a phone call from a couple that wanted to come right over and see the house. I started to tell them no because I was so exhausted and my husband wasn't home. But they said, "Oh, please! We're just right around the corner, and we can be right there." Then all of the sudden, I could sense the Holy Spirit was telling me to let them come over. Well, praise God that I obeyed because they wanted to buy the house. They had ten thousand dollars to put down, and they had already been working with a bank to get pre-approved. Not only did God do all of that for us, but He also sold our home for an outstanding price of eighty-seven thousand dollars. We ended up making a profit of almost forty thousand dollars. God was really giving me some awesome faith-building experiences through all of this. He showed me that if I would just step out in faith and do my part, He would show up and do His part.

Twenty-Four Days Passed

It was almost time to close on our old house, and I was still having trouble finding a bank that would finance our new home. Our credit still wasn't great, so I was going to have to try to put the house in just my name. Five banks told me no, and some lending institution said they might consider it at a high interest rate. I started thinking, *Lord, this just isn't funny. I know You want to give me a new home, but I can't find a lender.* I only had a few days left before we had to sign over the house to the new owners. I started to panic and thought, *Well, I'd rather stay in the house we're in than walk away and have no home to go to.*

The Night God Shook My House

It was about 6:00 p.m., and I was home alone. My mom was going to bring the kids home in a little while. I started praying and asking God for wisdom and guidance for my situation. I wanted to watch one of my favorite preachers who was about to come on TV. I must have dozed off while I was waiting because, all of the sudden, I awoke to loud thunder. When I looked out the window, it was storming really hard. Well, storms don't bother me, so I dozed back off in the recliner. Again I was woken up, and this time it felt like my house was shaking. I thought, *Oh no, we're having an earthquake.* Then I thought, *Wait*

9

a minute! I live in Michigan. That doesn't happen here.

I was so scared that I couldn't even move. By this time, the show I wanted to see was starting, and it was about Noah's ark. I thought, *Lord, are You trying to wake me up to watch this? Because if You are, You've got my fullest attention.* The preacher was talking about how Noah let God close the door of the ark without knowing where God was leading him or how long the journey would take. Noah loved and trusted God enough that he knew that no matter what, everything would be all right. When the preacher finished, I thought, *Well, God, that was interesting.* I didn't quite understand what this message had to do with my life and the situation I was faced with.

The Next Day

I told a precious, spirit-filled friend of mine, Theresa, that I didn't want to close on my house, because I still couldn't find a bank to finance me and would rather have the house I currently lived in than have no house. Then I began to share with her what happened to me the night before.

"Don't you get it?" she said.

"Get what?"

"God wants you to trust Him and let go of what's in your hand, so He can give you what's in His hand," she said. She told me to walk out of my house and put my faith and trust in God to make a way. Now, I had to think about this for a minute. I knew

I served a miracle-working God, but I was a fairly new Christian, and this seemed like the biggest step of faith that I'd ever been asked to take. Then God brought back to memory all the times He had come through for me.

Walking Away

We walked out of our house on a Saturday, exactly twenty-eight days after our first showing. We went to stay with my parents. That Monday, I received a call from the seventh bank telling me that they would finance me and give me a good interest rate. I was so excited and thanked Jesus over and over for waking me up that one night to hear the message on Noah's ark and for having my friend interpret the meaning. God was showing me that whatever I was willing to walk away from would determine what He could walk me into. I almost missed a huge blessing because I was focused on the fact that things weren't looking good for me in the natural world, but God had everything under control in the spiritual realm. God says, "Trust in the Lord with all your heart, and lean not on your own understanding; In all your ways acknowledge him, and He shall direct your paths" (Proverbs 3:5-6 NKJV).

Getting My Job Upgraded

This next faith-building experience changed my life drastically. The year was

1997, and I was promoted to a different department at the company I work for. The women on this referral team had been trying since 1994 to get this position upgraded to a higher level, which would mean a pay raise, but their request kept being denied. So, they decided to try one last time. About two weeks before it was time to present our case to our human resources department, some of the women got scared and wanted to postpone our meeting. They wanted to wait until a later time and see if our management would submit it for us. They didn't feel like they could take any more rejection.

All of sudden, I heard the Holy Spirit say to me, "Let's go and present this case." I thought, *Are You crazy? Be quiet! Just pipe down! Don't even go there; You know how terrified I am of speaking in front of people. You can just forget about that idea! There's no way I'm going to do that.* Before I knew what was happening, my mouth opened and out came the words, "I'll do it!" I couldn't believe what I was hearing. I thought, *Holy Spirit, what are You trying to do? Kill me? You know how scared I get. My heart starts racing so fast, and I feel like I could drop dead of a heart attack.*

One of my co-workers looked at me and said, "I really wish you would wait for management." I heard the Holy Spirit say to me, "Tell the girls they've tried it their way before. Now let's try it God's way." After I told them that, they just stood there looking at me as if I had just fallen off the wagon and bumped my head. Now, up until this point in my life, I had never really spoken about God with boldness at work. I guess I was too afraid of what my co-workers would think. From that moment on, the Holy Spirit really began to deal with me and teach me how to walk by faith, not by sight.

Preparing for the Presentation

I was still in shock that I agreed to do this. I had never given a presentation at work. The Holy Spirit had me pray over my notebook before I started doing any writing. So I did just that; I prayed over it. Not only was I terrified about giving this presentation, but I also hated to write. When I was in high school, I hated English and received a D in that class four years in a row.

Every night for two weeks, I would write and rewrite the presentation. So did one of my co-workers Theresa, who is a spirit-filled woman of God. Some of the other women got the charts and graphs ready. When we were finished, I was amazed at what an awesome job God did on this presentation.

The Big Day Had Arrived

A few days later, the time came to present our case. My boss, a few faith-filled co-workers, and I prayed in agreement that

God would soften the hearts of our human resource department. About five minutes before I was supposed to walk in the room, the co-worker who asked me not to do this showed up and said she would help me give the presentation. I thought, *Praise God!* She had been in the department a lot longer than I and could offer more insight into what changes had taken place over the years.

A few minutes into our presentation, human resources complimented us on the packet we had put together to present. They said it was one of the best they had ever seen. Little did they know that God had put it together; anything God puts His hand to will be awesome. Well, they all agreed we deserved an upgrade. *Thank You, Jesus.* Now we just had to convince middle and upper management of the same thing. The final step would be for the president of our company to also agree.

The Waiting Period

Over the next two months, we kept praying and believing that God's Word is true. Matthew 21:22 says, "And whatever things you ask in prayer, believing, you will receive" (NKJV).

One night, I was watching a preacher on a Christian television station, and he was speaking about Isaiah 41:10-13, where God says,

> *Fear not, for I am with you;* Be not dismayed, for I am your God. I will

strengthen you, *Yes, I will help you,* I will uphold you with My righteous right hand. Behold, all those who were incensed against you shall be ashamed and disgraced; They shall be as nothing, And those who strive with you shall perish. You shall seek them and not find them—Those who contended with you. Those who war against you Shall be as nothing, As a nonexistent thing. For I, the LORD, your God, will hold your right hand, Saying to you, *"Fear not, I will help you."* (NKJV)

Being Attacked by Satan

The next day, I really felt that God wanted me to take my Bible to work, make copies of those Scriptures from Isaiah, and give a copy to each of the women in my department. God knew I was about to be attacked that morning. A few hours into my morning, the battle began. People were coming against me left and right about the upgrade issue. I started feeling down, but then the Holy Spirit reminded me to read those Scriptures in Isaiah. So I did. He kept telling me, "You're doing the right thing. This is just an attack from Satan." My co-workers started getting really nervous that we weren't going to get the raise. I reminded them to read those Scriptures that God had me give to them.

God told me to reassure them that He says, "No weapon formed against you shall prosper, And every tongue which rises against you in judgment You shall condemn. This is the heritage of the servants of the Lord, And their righteousness is from Me" (Isaiah 54:17 NKJV). God promises that He will never leave us nor forsake us.

Speaking Out Boldly

I began to realize that the bolder I was about speaking God's Word, the more He would show up and move the situation in our favor. I had learned to step out in faith and believe that God would get this upgrade for us. I would be lying if I told you that I wasn't scared. I knew if we didn't get the raise that I would never hear the end of it. I had to keep telling my co-workers and myself that if God is for us, who can be against us? (Romans 8:31.) I was being attacked by many negative people, so I prayed and asked Jesus to strengthen me to stand against Satan's attacks of doubt and unbelief. I felt like I was the blind leading the blind.

This became the most challenging thing I'd ever done as a new Christian. It was completely out of character for me to stand boldly and speak about the power of God.

My friend came up to me one day and told me that a woman from another department had told her that we would never get the upgrade. Instantly, the Holy Spirit said, "Say that the woman just doesn't realize that God is on our team, and He's never lost a battle yet."

The Final Decision

A few more months passed, and then one day we received a phone call from management asking us to attend a meeting. I was so nervous. I knew the unbelievers were just dying for a chance to say, "I told you so, Tracy." We all sat down, and they informed us that we got the upgrade. Praise God! What an awesome moment that was to give God all the glory and praise that He was due. Not only did we end up getting the raise, but we also received back pay. Isn't that just like God to go above and beyond what you're hoping for?

What's so funny about this whole situation is that what started out over money ended up being something so much greater. It was an opportunity to stand up, boldly speak the name of Jesus, and demonstrate that all things are possible with God if we'll just believe. This experience showed the non-believers that God is real and faithful to the faithful. The one woman who had given me a hard time even apologized to me.

Blessings

Always try to remember that when Satan is fighting you the hardest, it's because he's afraid something good is about to happen.

He knows that if he can get you off track, you'll miss out on the Lord's blessings. God has so many blessings waiting for all of us, but we've got to have faith to believe them before we receive them. When God tells you to do something, no matter how crazy it might sound, just *do it*!

Prayer

Dear heavenly Father, help me to have enough faith to believe that all things are possible with You, no matter what situation I'm facing. Also, help me to realize that just because something looks impossible in the natural realm doesn't mean You're not doing something in the spiritual realm. Help me believe that You have everything under control; trust in You, Lord, with all my heart; and lean not on my own understanding. I know You can make a way where there seems to be none!

Chapter 2

God Cares about Every Area
of Our Lives

God truly does care about the smallest
details in our lives. If you'll let Him,
He wants to get involved in every area of
your life. I know we tend to think God is
too busy to be bothered with our trivial
day-to-day functions, but that's not so.
No matter how big or small your problem
is, He wants to help. He loves us so much
that whatever concerns us also concerns
Him. God taught me this lesson when I was
in desperate need of some help.

God Decorates My Kitchen

It was Monday, February 13, 2000, around
10:30 p.m. I was talking to God about a
get-together that I would be hosting at
my house on Saturday, February 18, 2000.
I said, "Lord, I really need some help
with decorating my kitchen." I had only

been living in my new house for about
five months, and I still hadn't done
anything to the kitchen. I really don't
care for shopping, which is probably why
I hadn't decorated yet. I was telling God
how great it would be if He could have
the sister of a co-worker of mine help
me out. I knew she was a great decorator
because she would always make up beautiful
flower arrangements and bring them into
work to sell.

The next day, that lady unexpectedly
stopped in to see her sister while I was
visiting also. I was so excited! I thought,
"Lord, You're the greatest!" We started to
talk, and I explained my dilemma. She was
so sweet and offered to help me out. She
said I could come over to her house the
next day to get some ideas. To my surprise
when I arrived, she had made me up some of
the most beautiful flower arrangements for
my kitchen. I was so happy that I bought
them all.

Now I was still in need of some other
items, such as rugs, a canister set,
placemats, and some colored bottles to put
on top of my cupboards. I had been running
all over town, frantically trying to find
these items, but I just couldn't seem to
find anything that caught my eye. Time was
running out for me.

Shopping Trip with the Lord

Friday morning, God woke me up fifteen
minutes before my alarm was set to go off.

He told me to go to a store called Meijer's on Hill Road. I thought, *How odd! I never go to that Meijer's.* I said, "Lord, I've already been to the other two Meijer stores this week and couldn't find what I was looking for."

"Yes I know," He said, "but you need to hurry up and get ready so you can stop at this one before you go to work."

I thought, *Okay!* And I did just that. Not only did they have everything I wanted, but it was all on sale. The reason He told me to go before work was because they only had one blue canister set left in the style I wanted. Also, they only had five light blue bottles, and that was exactly how many I needed. Praise God! I thought, *Lord, You never cease to amaze me. You care about every detail of our lives.* I began to cry and say, "Thank You, Jesus."

I guess I had just always assumed the Lord had more important things to do than take me shopping. You see, that day God showed me how He's never too busy to take time out for His children. That really made me stop and think, *why do I act like I'm too busy for Him sometimes?* You see, as a child of God, I know He loves us so much. He wants to help, no matter how trivial we think our problem or need is!

Getting My Taxes Done

After the shopping incident, God showed me again how much He cares and that He really does hear our prayers. He has the answer! If we could only learn to take every concern or problem to Him first, a lot of unnecessary headaches could be avoided—as you'll see in this next story.

It was tax season, and I was in desperate need of a good return. So the night before my husband (now ex-husband) and I were supposed to go get our taxes done, we started frantically looking all over the house for everything we were to take with us. Now don't ask me why, but for some reason we always seemed to wait until the last minute to gather up all our information. Pretty stupid! Then we always played the blame game, accusing each other of losing important documents. While we were in a heated debate over who was at fault, we then realized that we both had claimed too many exemptions on our paychecks. Needless to say, the debate got a little hotter!

While we were going over everything that we could find, we discovered there was a good possibility that we'd owe about $2,500. Now by this point, we were no longer in a debate. World War III broke out between us.

Finally, after we managed to calm down and apologize to one another, we then did what we should have done in the first place: *pray!* We started asking God to help us not to owe. In fact, we needed to get back about $2,500 because we had some overdue bills that desperately needed to be paid. Owing just wasn't an option, as our bank account was completely empty. Like that was a surprise! For a long time, it seemed we could never break even, and we forgot about trying to get ahead because that was just downright laughable.

The next day at work, I was talking to some of my friends about what I was asking God to do for us. They started cracking up! One of them said, "Seriously, Tracy, what are you going to do about this money you're probably going to owe?"

I said, "I already told you what I am going to do: *pray* for a miracle!"

My friends just kept laughing at me and said, "Oh! Okay. If we see you crying when you come back, then we'll try to help you to come up with a more realistic plan." You see, I was a new Christian, and these friends of mine weren't Christians. I was really scared! I was just learning how to have faith in God.

Later that day, when I came back from getting my taxes done, the girls said, "Well how much do you owe?"

"You're not going to believe this," I said. "We're getting back $2,423."

They said, "Shut up! You're lying!"

I said, "I'm telling you the truth." They were so amazed, and frankly, so was I.

It stunned me to think that if we just go to God first and have faith in Him, He can work it all out! No problem is too big for God. He has the answer to every situation that we're facing. He wants to get involved in every area of our lives. Don't ever think that He's too busy for you. He loves you!

Prayer

Dear Jesus, thank You for caring about every area of my life. Thank You for never being too busy to get involved in everything that concerns me. Lord, I pray that I always remember to take time out of my day to spend with You. You are so precious and deserve my fullest attention. Help me to remember to always put You first in my life. I love You so much. You're an awesome God, and it's a privilege to be one of Your children.

Chapter 3

You Can Never Out-Give God

Don't ever be afraid to give to the Lord. He's not trying to take anything from you. He's trying to give something to you. Until you're willing to release what's in your hand, God can't release what's in His. Please trust Him! What's in His hand will always be greater than what is in yours!

For a long time, I never understood what it meant to tithe and give an offering until my husband (now ex-husband) and I started attending church faithfully. I began to write out a simple little check each week, and I do mean little. As time went on, I learned that God expects us to give the first 10 percent of our paychecks as our tithe-not what's left over after we pay everyone else. Now, an offering doesn't always have to be money. It can be your time or something else that would bring glory to God. Not only does God bless your finances, but He also blesses other areas of your life.

Testing God with Your Finances

In Malachi 3:8, God says, *"Will a man rob God? Yet you have robbed Me! But you say, In what way have we robbed You? In tithes and offerings"* (NKJV)). He clearly tells us in verses 9 and 10 to *test Him* in this area and see if He doesn't open up the windows of heaven and pour out such a blessing that there will not be room enough to receive it. This is the only time in the Bible that He tells us to test Him.

Withholding What Rightfully Belongs to God

I told my husband I wanted to start tithing and giving offerings. He said that would be fine. As I began to give, amazing things happened to me. Now my husband, on the other hand, wasn't quite ready to give up his money to God.

One Sunday afternoon our cars were parked side by side at home, when all of a sudden our three-year-old son decided to throw a pool ball that he had found in the garage. Well, guess whose windshield took a big crack? My husband's! He was so angry. I asked him, "Why are you so angry at our son?"

He replied, "This is going to cost me one hundred dollars."

I reminded him that he robbed God of a $120 in tithe money earlier at church. "God is just repaying you for robbing Him," I said.

"Yeah! You're probably right."

Becoming a Faithful Tither

Well, I finally talked my husband into becoming a faithful tither. He only got paid twice a month because he was a life insurance agent. His paychecks weren't always the same amount because it all depended on how much he had sold prior to getting paid. I needed exactly seven hundred dollars each pay period to pay his portion of our bills. Well, wouldn't you know it? His first check was exactly seven hundred dollars. Oh, great! Now what are we going to do? I said, "Give God 10 percent."

"If I do that, we won't be able to pay some of these bills," he said. I told him that we needed to just trust that the Lord would provide. Another pay period came, and we had an exact repeat of the last one. By this point, he was starting to get frustrated. However, he decided to give to God what rightfully belonged to Him.

We started this in January of 1999. By June of 1999, his paycheck had climbed all the way up to $2,400 every pay period. Praise God! But wait just a minute: here comes the twist! In July, my husband decided that tithing was getting too expensive. He was paying $240 in tithes and $50 in offerings every pay period. The whole month of July, he paid nothing to the Lord. Well, in the first week of August, my husband gave $800 to a guy he barely knew as a down payment on a new furnace that we needed. That guy cashed our check, and we never received our furnace.

My husband was so angry. I asked him, "Why are you so mad at him?"

"Because he just stole my money. I trusted him!"

I said, "Well isn't that exactly what you just did to God the whole month of July?"

"Yeah, but this guy promised."

I politely reminded him that he also made a promise to our Lord and Savior. After he finally calmed down, he realized that he should just let the guy keep the money. The guy was extremely poor, and his wife and children were in need of some things.

From August to March of 2000, he continued robbing God, and his checks dropped all the way down to $350 every pay period. It just doesn't pay to rob God!

Giving God 20 Percent

One day I was reading a book called *Wisdom and Money*. The author said we should always pray for wisdom, because without it, we can make some really bad choices. We should also give God the first 10 percent of our pay and then put 20 percent into our savings.

Instantly a thought came into my head. What if I did the reverse and gave God the first 20 percent and only saved 10? I thought, *You can never go wrong in giving your finances to the Lord.* Well, a week later I received my check, and greed took over. I only gave God 10 percent, and I put the other 20 percent into my savings. Six weeks passed, and it occurred to me that my savings account was completely empty. I had needed to keep withdrawing the money for one reason or another.

Now, up until this point, I hadn't told anyone about this idea. So one day, I decided to tell my husband about what happened. I asked him if he thought God planted that idea into my mind. He said, "Well that's a possibility!" A couple more weeks passed, and I just couldn't forget it. I went back to my husband and explained to him that I really felt like God wanted us to do this. He agreed that maybe we should do it.

We started following the plan in March of 2000 and continued doing it until the end of June. Amazing things started happening to us. God's blessings were chasing us down and overtaking us. God gave my husband so much favor in his job that people were calling us to purchase insurance from him instead of him having to do all the calling. He sold over thirty-eight thousand dollars worth of insurance in those three months, which was not common in such a short amount of time. He won "agent of the month" awards. Not only did God do all this, but also my husband qualified for the trip to

Disney World that his company was going on in August. Praise God! Our five-year-old son was so excited about going.

You Can Never Out-Give God

Unfortunately, due to a tragic turn of events the remainder of my journey in learning to walk by faith was without my first husband. My husband struggled deeply with wanting to serve the Lord and the temptations of the world. The Bible tells us in 1 Peter 5 8:9 *"Be sober, be vigilant; because your adversary the devil walks about like a roaring lion, seeking whom he may devour. Resist him, steadfast in the faith, knowing that the same sufferings are experienced by your brotherhood in the world."* (NKJV)

It was around August of the year 2000 that he became addicted to drugs again for the 3rd time in our marriage. I tried desperately to get him to stop, but he wouldn't. My heart was so broken. I never wanted my children to grow up in a split family. But, by March of 2001 I finally made the painful and heartbreaking decision to divorce him because it was no longer a safe environment for my children and me to be living in the same house with him.

The drugs would cause him to behave in ways that were out of character for him. For instance sometimes he would become violent with me. His explosive temper terrified me. I knew that I couldn't let our boy's grow up in this type of atmosphere. I didn't want them to think that it was ok to do drugs and to be physically, mentally abusive to women. It was around Easter of 2001, and I had just started going through my divorce a month earlier. I was having such a hard time trying to make ends meet, and my child support still wasn't set up. I worked fourteen hours of overtime and took nine exemptions one week to pay the house payment and car payment, which were both overdue! After paying those payments, I only had a little bit of money left. I still needed to buy my sons' Easter candy and my youngest son's birthday present. I thought, *Oh, God, please help!*

I had missed Sunday's service the week before Easter. On that Wednesday at church, I knew I needed to pay God my tithe money from the previous Sunday. Then I remembered I had forgotten to mail in my fifty-dollar monthly pledge to TCT, a Christian TV station. I thought, *Well, God will understand if I keep this money just this one time and spend the money on my kids.* But as the day went on, the Holy Spirit kept dealing with me on how that money belongs to the Lord. By the end of day, I couldn't take it any longer. I felt like I was carrying around stolen money. Now, I know God wouldn't have been mad at me if I had decided not to, but I decided to take a leap of faith and write out both checks.

When I got home that day and checked my mailbox, there sat a check for $289. The state had decided to return some of our income tax that they had taken from us earlier that year. I thought, *Thank You, Jesus! I'm so glad I decided not to cheat You.* The next day when I got to work, someone laid $150 on my desk. I was so excited! I just kept thanking God. Well, not only did God do all that for me, but two days later my brothers Mike and Jeff gave me $250 for no reason. I was so grateful that the Holy Spirit had talked me into giving up what was in my hand so that I could receive what was in God's hand. As if all of this wasn't enough, I also received another unexpected check for $225 from a cell phone company I used to have. They said I had overpaid a year before. Then, on that Monday, my friends Niki and Alisa brought me a dozen roses and a $50 gift certificate to the mall.

I gave God $100, and He gave me $964. That just goes to prove that you can never out-give God.

Prayer

Dear Lord Jesus, I pray that I always put my trust in You. Help me to never take what rightfully belongs to You. Help me to realize all that I am and all that I have is from You. Also, help me to never be afraid to let go of what's in my hand to receive what's in Your hand. I pray I always have enough faith and trust in You to know You're not trying to take something from me; You're trying to give something to me. I believe Your word is true in 2 Corinthians 9:6: "But this I say: He who sows sparingly will also reap sparingly, and he who sows bountifully will also reap bountifully" (NKJV). I thank You, Jesus, for the opportunity to give back to You. You have done so much for me; You lay down Your life so that I may have life. Words could never express my gratitude. I love You!

Chapter 4

God Is in Control of Your Finances

Don't look at your current circumstances and think, *Well, this is it. I'm financially ruined. I'm about to lose everything I've been working so hard for. My house payments are falling way behind, and my car is one step away from being repossessed. Things are looking pretty bleak right now in the natural world.* You might even be thinking bankruptcy is the only way out of the mess you're in, but wait! The world's way isn't God's way. In the supernatural world, God will work things out if you'll just walk by faith and not by sight (2 Corinthians 5:7).

I was faced with this very situation in March of 2001 when my life as I knew it flipped upside down. I was going through an extremely painful divorce, and my finances were quickly spiraling out of control.

When my husband left, he only took his clothes, leaving behind everything else—including all the debt he had acquired.

Almost everything we owned was in my name, so it didn't take long before my phone started ringing off the hook. The bill collectors were putting so much pressure on me. I was scared! I thought, *Oh, Lord, what am I going to do?* I knew I didn't make enough money to cover everything.

Refusing to File for Bankruptcy

By June of 2001, my bills were far behind, and my back was against the wall. I had worked all the overtime that was offered and still couldn't make ends meet. So many people kept trying to talk me into filing for bankruptcy. I had a real problem with that being the solution. My spirit just wouldn't allow me to buy into the lie that I was financially ruined. I just kept telling myself, "I serve a big God who walks on streets of gold and owns everything in this world." I knew that in the natural world, I was a sinking ship. Time was running out for me. So, I just kept praying and asking, "God, please make a way where there seems to be no way." His word says, "If God is for us, who can be against us?" (Romans 8:31 NKJV). Truthfully, I was really scared, but I knew my loving heavenly Father cared about every detail of my life.

The First Challenge

The first big challenge I faced was trying to unload a brand new Monte Carlo that my husband had talked me into purchasing one year earlier. He also had me put the car in my name. The payment was over four hundred dollars a month. I knew there was no way I could afford to keep it. I decided to detail the car myself and put it up for sale. This wasn't going to be easy, because he had put over sixty thousand miles on it, and I still owed eighteen thousand dollars.

Time was running out. The bank informed me that it would be repossessing the car soon. I didn't want that to happen, because I knew the bank would run it through an auction and bill me for the balance of around ten thousand dollars. I thought, *Oh, Lord, I'm in deep trouble and need Your help once again.*

I decided to take the car up to VG's grocery store on a Saturday to see if maybe I could sell it over the weekend. Sunday at 2:00, my mom and I were taking my kids to play at the McDonald's right by VG's grocery store. On our way home about two hours later, I noticed the car was gone. I said, "Mom where is the car?"

"I don't know," she said. "Maybe your dad came and got it."

When we got back to her house, I said, "Dad, where is the car?"

"What are you talking about?" he asked.

By this point, I started to panic. I wasn't sure if the car had been stolen or repossessed. Either way, I knew this wasn't going to be easy to explain to the police.

Suspicion at the Police Station

Well, I know what you must be thinking: how is she going to explain this? When I got to the police station and tried to explain that I wasn't sure what had happened to the car, they treated me like I had stolen it. I became their prime suspect. After I left, I said, "Lord, I'm really in trouble now."

The next day I called the bank and asked if they had taken the car. They said no. I couldn't believe it. Somebody had the nerve to steal the car in broad daylight. Well, a week later the car turned up completely stripped and cut in half. By this point, the police really started giving me a hard time. They told me they would be investigating me. I was stunned. I couldn't believe this was happening. My brother Bob kept teasing me about how boring my life is. He said, "I feel sorry for the person who has to follow you around. The only places you go are to work and church." Well, just when you think things can't get any worse, I found out who stole the car. It was a person I went to high school with. Praise God, I was finally cleared of any wrongdoing.

Fighting with the Insurance Company

However, there was still one problem. Because I was honest with the insurance company and admitted how many miles were on the car, the company wouldn't pay off the total balance to the bank. The company wanted to do its own investigation. By this point, I was so frustrated. The bank kept breathing down my neck, wanting its money.

I can remember one day crying out to God and telling Him that I just couldn't take all the pressure anymore. I said, "Lord, between fighting with all the different bill collectors and trying to work tons of overtime, plus trying to go through all the stress of my marriage breaking up—not to mention trying to take care of my two precious little boys—I think I'm going to have a complete meltdown. Then I remembered God that says, "Take My yoke upon you and learn from Me, for I am gentle and lowly in heart, and you will find rest for souls. For My yoke is easy and My burden is light" (Mathew 11:29-30 NKJV)

Two days later the insurance company called and said, "They would pay off all, but $1,500." Praise God, that's better than $10,000.

GOD SAVES ME FROM BANKRUPTCY

I wasn't out of the woods yet. My overhead was still too high. No matter how hard I tried I still couldn't make ends meet. Those bill collectors were hot on my trail. I cried to God once again and said; "Lord I've done all that I know to do." I don't know what else I can do to avoid bankruptcy. However, I knew I served a big God and no problem was too big for Him. I said, "Lord it's been bad enough my children have endured the pain of losing their father. Please don't let them lose their home too." All things are possible with God, no matter how hopeless the situation seems.

The night before I had to make a decision about what to do, my heavenly Father had my earthly father come to my rescue. What was so amazing about this was that two years earlier, my dad had fallen in the shop where he worked and injured his knee so badly that he'd had to retire. For two years, he fought with his employer to settle up with him. He finally received his check and was able to bless me with enough money to get me up on my feet. My dad said, "God saw that you were going to be in trouble and that I would have to help you. I don't think it's any accident that I fell, because if it weren't for this settlement, I couldn't have helped you." I'll never forget that because my dad isn't even a Christian, yet he recognized the power of God moving in the situation.

My point is this: God is no respecter of persons. What He did for me, He'll do for you. So don't worry about what to do when you're facing difficult times and your back is against the wall. Just call upon your Father in heaven. Trust in Him to make a way where there isn't a way. Don't give up; you can make it. I know it gets hard sometimes, but in those times God wants to show Himself strong in your life.

Prayer

Dear heavenly Father, I thank You for being in control of my finances. I thank You that no matter what situation I'm facing, I can turn to You. No problem is too big for You. I pray that I always use godly wisdom to handle my finances. I pray that I can learn how to live free of burdensome debt. Show me how to increase my finances, not decrease them. May I always be paid well for the work I do, and may the money I make never be stolen, lost, devoured, destroyed, or wasted. Thank You for always watching over me and turning my test into my testimony.

Chapter 5

God Will Supply for All Your Needs

While I was going through my divorce, money was extremely tight, and God taught me another important lesson in walking by faith. When He says in Mathew 6:25-34. "Do not worry," He means just that. In verses 25-27, He says, "Therefore I tell you, do not worry about your life, what you will eat or drink; or about your body, what you will wear. Is not life more important than food, and the body more important than clothes? Look at the birds of the air; they do not sow or reap or store away in barns, and yet your heavenly Father feeds them. Are you not much more valuable than they? Who of you by worrying can add a single hour to his life?" (NIV).

Don't be afraid to put your trust in Him, even when your current circumstances suggest that it's hopeless and you can't see how or when God will supply your needs.

He can make a way where there seems to be none. That's exactly what He did in these next few stories.

In Need of Some Food

I was headed home from work one day, feeling very distraught about my finances and talking to God about a dilemma I was having. I only had $1.36, and payday was two days away. I said, "Lord, I don't have anything to take to work to eat for the next two days, and I don't have anything at the house for the boys to snack on." As a parent, it really bothered me that I couldn't afford to keep our home stocked up. My parents were awesome; they would always feed my kids dinner before I picked them up, but then later in the evening they always wanted a little snack before bed.

As I was pulling in my driveway, I noticed my friend Carrie pulling in behind me. I said, "Girl, what are you doing here?"

"Well, as I was leaving work, I just felt compelled to stop at the store and pick up a few items for the boys and you," she said.

I was so stunned! My mouth dropped wide open. God had her pick me up two days' worth of lunches for me and some snacks for the boys.

The boys were so excited, and I began to cry. She said, "What's wrong?"

I said, "You're not going to believe this, but I was just talking to God about my need for these exact items." Then she began to cry. I was so thankful that she was willing to obey the voice of God and not think up a hundred reasons why she shouldn't stop at the store. I thought, *Lord, You're amazing! You're always right on time.*

Needing Some Milk and Cereal

One evening about 9:00 p.m., I realized I didn't have anything to feed my children for breakfast. I was so troubled by this, because I was doing everything I could to keep from going under financially. After paying all the bills, there never seemed to be any money left to buy groceries. I said, "Lord, You see that I'm a faithful tither and giver and that I'm trying my very best to keep up with everything. Your Word says in Philippians 4:19, 'And my God shall supply all your need according to His riches in glory by Christ Jesus'" (NKJV).

People kept trying to talk me into lowering the amount I gave God each month, but I just couldn't see that as the solution. God has always been so faithful to me, and I didn't want to take what rightfully belonged to Him. I knew this was just an attack from Satan to get me to put my trust in the world instead of my heavenly Father. I also knew that the world's way isn't God's way. I had to learn to trust in Him.

My parents had always told me I could come to them anytime I had a need. However,

I hated to burden them all the time with all of my problems. I felt like they already did their job in raising my brothers and I, and now it was time to stand on my own two feet. I also didn't think it should be their responsibility to pick up the slack for my ex-husband, who still wasn't paying his child support.

Around 9:30 p.m., I heard a knock on the door. I thought, *Who is knocking at my door this late on a work night?* To my surprise, there stood Marie, a precious woman of God whom I went to church with. We only lived a few of miles from each other, but she had never come over before. I said, "Marie, what are you doing here?"

"Well, it's the strangest thing; I was in the grocery store getting some milk and cereal for my little ones. Then all of the sudden I felt God was telling me to get some for you, too. So here I am."

I said, "Marie, thank you so much for obeying God. I was just crying out to Him earlier and telling Him I was in need of these items." I knew this was a huge inconvenience to her because her husband and two small children were waiting for her to get home.

I think what touched me the most about this was the fact that God heard my cry for help. Sometimes we can feel like we're all alone to deal with our problems, but that's not true. God is always right there to meet our every need. No problem is too big for Him. That just proved to me once again that His word is true when He says, "I will never leave you nor forsake you."

Someone Else in Need of Milk

I heard a story once about someone else in need of milk. A young man had been to a Wednesday night Bible study. The pastor had shared about listening to God and obeying His voice. The young man couldn't help but wonder, *Does God still speak to people?* After service, he went out with some friends for coffee and pie to discuss the service. Several different friends talked about how God had led them in different ways.

It was about ten o'clock when the young man started driving home. Sitting in his car, he just began to pray, "God, if You still speak to people, speak to me. I will listen. I will do my best to obey." As he drove down the main street of his town, he had the strangest thought to stop and buy a gallon of milk. He shook his head and said out loud, "God, is that You?" He didn't get a reply. He started toward home, but again the thought to buy a gallon of milk popped into his head. The young man thought about Samuel and how he didn't recognize the voice of God and how little Samuel ran to Eli. "Okay, God, in case that is You, I will buy the milk." It didn't seem like too hard of a test of obedience to him. He thought, *I could always use the milk.*

He stopped and purchased the gallon of milk and started off toward home. As he passed Seventh Street, he again felt the urge, "Turn down that street." *This is crazy*, he thought, and drove on past the intersection. Again, he felt that he should turn down Seventh Street. At the next intersection he turned back and headed down Seventh. Half jokingly, he said out loud, "Okay, God, I will."

He drove several blocks, when suddenly he felt like he should stop. He pulled over to the curb and looked around. He was in a semi-commercial area of town. It wasn't the best, but it wasn't the worst of neighborhoods, either. The businesses were closed, and most of the houses looked dark, as if people were already in bed. Again, he sensed something: "Go and give milk to the people in the house across the street."

The young man looked at the house. It was dark, and it looked liked the people were either gone or already asleep. He started to open the door and then sat back in the car seat. He thought, *Lord, this is insane. Those people are asleep, and if I wake them up they are going to be mad and I will look stupid.* Again, he felt like he should go and give the milk. Finally, he opened the door. "Okay, God," he said. "If this is You, I will go to the door, and I will give them the milk. If You want me to look like a crazy person, I want to be obedient. I guess that will count for something, but if they don't answer right away, I am out of here."

He walked across the street and rang the bell. He could hear some noise inside. A man's voice yelled out, "Who is it? What do you want?" Then the door opened before the young man could get away. The man was just standing there in his jeans and T-shirt. He looked like he just got out of bed. He had a strange look on his face, and he didn't seem too happy to have a stranger standing on his doorstep. "What is it?" The young man thrust out the gallon of milk, "Here, I brought this to you." The man took the milk and rushed down a hallway. Then from down the hall came a woman carrying the milk toward the kitchen. The man was following her, holding a baby. The baby was crying. The man had tears streaming down his face. Then the man began speaking and half-crying, "We were just praying. We had some big bills this month and ran out of money. We didn't have any milk for our baby. I was just praying and asking God to show me how to get some milk."

His wife was in the kitchen and yelled out, "I asked Him to send an angel with some. Are you an angel?" The young man reached into his wallet and pulled out all the money he had and put it into the man's hand, and then he turned and walked back to his car with tears streaming down his face. He knew that God still answered prayers.

In Need of Some Deodorant

My morning started out like any other morning. I was racing around the house, trying to get the kids and myself out the door on time, when I reached for my deodorant and discovered that it was all gone. I thought, *Oh, great, just one more thing I'm in need of and don't have the extra money to buy.* So, I did what any other desperate person in my situation would have done: I scraped and dug at it until I had enough to smell decent for the day. I'm pretty sure that a lot of people have done this and then later a bought a new one, but the real burn was that I didn't dare throw it away because I didn't know when I could buy more.

I almost had to laugh at myself because I thought, *How could this be happening to me? I grew up in a middle class family."* I never dreamed as a little girl that I would grow up to be a deodorant digger. It was a real eye opener for me that not everyone can just run up to the store when they're out of something. My whole life I would hear my mom say to my dad, "Ken, I need you to go to the store," when we were out of a certain item. I had no idea as a child what the real world went through. My parents didn't have a lot of money, but we never seemed to go without the bare necessities. Later I realized that God needed to allow me to go through a difficult situation so that He could develop compassion in me for others. I know He didn't cause my situation, but He used it to build character in me. I was spoiled rotten and didn't even realize it.

As I was driving to work, I thought, *Oh, Lord, when is this nightmare going to end?* I was doing everything I knew to do to keep us afloat, and I still couldn't make ends meet. By this point, I was so desperate for some relief that I thought, *I'd at least feel better if I could get the ends to come close and tie them together with a rope.*

Well, later that day, I forgot about my dilemma and headed off to church. When I arrived, a precious friend of mine, Gina, said, "After church, come with me out to my car." After the service was finished, she and I were walking to her car when she said, "The Lord told me to buy you a few things today. Now, I hope you don't get offended by this, but I really felt like He told me to get you some deodorant." I looked at her and said, "Girl, you're not going to believe this, but I ran out today and was talking to God about it." Then I asked her what brand she bought me—not that it mattered. I was thankful that she bought me some, but I was thinking, *I wonder if it's the same brand I ran out of.* She looked at me strangely and said, "Well, at first I was just going to get the cheap stuff because I didn't know what you liked, but then God told me to get you a specific brand, the Dove Fresh Scent." God is so awesome; that is exactly what I ran out of this morning. We stood there for a moment in awe of how awesome God is. We were truly amazed at how He will supply our every need. I gave her a hug and thanked her for being so obedient to the Lord. Now I can smell good again tomorrow.

On the way home, I just kept thanking the Lord for supplying my every need. I thought, *Lord, You even care about my hygiene.*

Needing Some Gas for the Week

Earlier that night at church, when it came time to take up the offering, I wanted so badly to give to God. However, the only money I had was the twenty dollars I had set aside to purchase my gas for the week to get back and forth to work. In the natural world, this would be a crazy thing to do, but I knew in my heart God had always been faithful to me and had never ever let me down. I decided to give God the whole twenty dollars and trust Him to somehow supply my need.

The next day at work, my friend Tammy laid twenty dollars on my desk. She said, "I really feel like God wants me to give you this." I began to cry and explained to her what had happened the night before. She was so excited that God had used her to bless someone else. She had just recently been through a hard time herself. I was so grateful that she was an awesome woman of God who was willing to obey Him.

But wait! God will never let you outdo Him. He went a few steps farther to bless my children and me. Later that day, my friend Janice told me to come over to her house because she had bought me a bunch of groceries. Then, when I got home, my dad paid my consumer bill in full, which came to $290, and my mom let me keep my daycare check of $150. I thought, *Lord, You are truly amazing! You took my last $20 and turned it into a whole lot more.* I couldn't help but wonder if none of this other stuff would have happened to me if I had held onto that little $20.

His word is true, and He clearly says in 2 Corinthians 9:6-7, "But this I say: he who sows sparingly will also reap sparingly, and he who sows bountifully will also reap bountifully. So let each one give as he purposes in his heart, not grudgingly or of necessity; *for God loves a cheerful giver*" (NKJV).

In Desperate Need of Some New Clothes

It was springtime, and the kids and I were in desperate need of some new summer clothes. I still wasn't getting my child support, and I just couldn't afford new clothes for us. I went to the Lord and said, "I don't know what to do. Can You please help us?" It wasn't a matter of want; it was a matter of need. The kids had outgrown everything.

Later that day, there was a knock on my door, and it was my precious older brother, Bob. He's the type that would give you the shirt off his back if you needed it. He started telling me how he and his girlfriend had broken up and he needed to return six hundred dollars worth of stuff to the store but couldn't find the receipt. The store told him he could exchange the merchandise for something else. "I decided to take you and the boys on a shopping spree and spoil you guys."

I said, "That sounds awesome, but why don't you buy yourself something?"

He said, "Oh, there's nothing I want." I stood there in total shock at how faithful God is.

You can truly take His word at face value. He means what He says when He tells us not worry about what we will eat, drink, or wear. He will supply all your needs and, a lot of times, even your desires. God is truly amazing! He is always right on time.

God wants to take your tests and turn them into your testimony. All that you're going through is just positioning you for where God is taking you. Tough times don't last, but tough people do. God has greater things for you tomorrow than what you went through yesterday. Change your way of thinking so God can change your way of living. *Trust in Him. He is the answer!*

Prayer

Dear God, thank You for always supplying all my needs. Your Word is so true. When You tell us, "Do not worry," You mean just that. I pray that I always listen to Your voice when You're telling me to help someone else in need. No matter how strange Your instructions may sound, I know Your ways are not our ways and Your thoughts are much higher than our thoughts. I pray I can always be a vessel You will use to bless to others. In Jesus' name, I pray.

Chapter 6

The Champion Hidden Within You

There's a champion hidden inside of each of us. Don't let your current circumstances define who you really are. This was my final lesson to learn after my divorce. I didn't know who I was anymore and what I could accomplish on my own. I was so used to hiding in the shadows of my husband's success that I never took the time to figure out who God created me to be. I needed God to help me to stir up my gifts and talents that He's hidden within me. Philippians 4:13 says, "I can do all things through Christ who strengthens me" (NKJV).

Now, maybe you're sitting there thinking, *What gifts or talents do I have?* Well, what job would you do for free if money weren't an issue? Ask yourself what you feel passionate about. What do people say are your strong points? It can be anything from being organized to being a good caretaker. People might say that you have a great personality and they enjoy talking with you. God has already equipped you with all the talent that you need to be a champion, but it's up to you to develop it. God can take your natural abilities and put His anointing on you so that you'll have His supernatural abilities working in you. He's already gone ahead of you and strategically placed everything and everyone in your path that you'll need. Now all you have to do is to believe it by faith. Ask God to burn the desires He wishes for you deep into your soul. Let God take control of your life. I promise you that you won't regret it. You will know such inner peace when you let God be in the driver's seat of your life. God thinks you're so special! It doesn't matter what negative things people have said about you. The only thing that matters is what God says, and He has plenty of awesome things to say about you.

Sometimes you may feel like life is just one big rat race that you're running in everyday. You may rush off to a job you can't stand only to find that you can barely make ends meet, and sometimes you don't even have enough to do that. It's not God's will for your life to be miserable day in and day out, thinking, *Well, I have to make a living, so this is probably as good as it gets for me.* No, you're missing it! God knows you have to earn a living, but He wants you to enjoy your journey through life. That's why He's built into your personality the qualities that would make you excellent at a certain job. God has an amazing plan for your life.

Think about how many times we run to and fro, frantically looking for happiness in all the wrong people, places, or things. That's the mistake I kept making. I already had everything I would ever need, and that was Jesus. I didn't need anything else to make me happy. I don't know why it took me so long to figure that out.

When people look at our lives, they should be able to see the favor of God all over us. It's God's will for us to be happy, healthy, and filled with His joy and peace that surpasses all understanding. God is counting on us to show the world that living for Him is the most exciting thing a person could ever do. This kind of true happiness and fulfillment can only be found when you're walking in the center of God's will for your life. Nothing else can even come close to the true peace and joy that you'll experience. True joy is not momentary and fleeting like the things of this world. Only the things done for Christ will last; everything else will pass away.

Sure, there will be trials, but with God on your side, you will come through the storms a much better person. With every test and trial comes a testimony. I'm living proof of that. While I was suffering my darkest hours of a broken heart and shattered dreams, God was already working things out in the supernatural realm for my good. Trust that God only has your best interest at heart, but also remember that nothing ventured leads to nothing gained. If you keep doing what you've been doing and expecting different results, that's the definition of insanity.

You didn't make it this far because you are wise. You made it because God's amazing grace and love for you kept you and sustained you. The Lord is constantly trying to grow us. He allows us to go through wilderness times so that we can learn to totally trust in Him. God has more for you today than what you went through yesterday. Let go, and let God be in charge. You won't regret it! Don't give up, and don't give in. Your miracle is on its way.

God Wants to Do a New Thing

Until your desire to go forward becomes greater than your memories of past pains and failures, you'll always live in yesterday's struggles. Isaiah 43:18-19 says, "Do not remember the former things, Nor, consider the things of old. Behold, I will do a new thing, Now, it shall spring forth: Shall you not know it? I will even make a road in the wilderness And rivers in the desert" (NKJV).

When you allow God to renew your mind and release you from fear, He can begin to move you toward your destiny. Exhale the old air, and inhale some new. God has more for you today than what you went through yesterday. An earthquake is coming into your prison, just as in the days of the apostle Paul. It's the midnight hour. Just keep praising God, and He'll break you out of the dungeons of your past and free you to become all He wants you to be.

Change can sometimes be a very difficult and painful process for our flesh. We can become so accustomed to the way things have always been that the thought of doing something new can seem frightening. Think about a caterpillar. In order to become a beautiful butterfly that can spread its wings and fly, it must first form a cocoon and go through all the necessary changes that have to take place. I'm sure that this can be a very unpleasant experience for the caterpillar, but once it's up in the air, flying from place to place and experiencing new things, I bet it never wants to go back to crawling around again.

Even when we know it's time for a change, sometimes the fear of the unknown can hold us back. 2 Timothy 1:7 says, "For God has not given us a spirit of fear, but of power and of love and of a sound mind" (NKJV). Nobody likes to step out blindly and walk by faith, but that's the very key to seeing your dreams become reality. It's no fun to let God take His Holy Spirit scissors and cut some junk out of our lives. But when He's finished, we're like that beautiful butterfly.

Getting Out of Our Comfort Zones

God is constantly trying to take us out our comfort zones so that we'll learn to totally trust in Him. Proverbs 3:5-6 says, "Trust in the Lord with all your heart and lean not on your own understanding; In all your ways acknowledge Him, And He shall direct your paths" (NKJV).

As I'm writing this chapter, I must admit that the Lord has taken me through so many changes over the last few years. That has been difficult for me at times, because it's hard for me to get out of my comfort zone. Normally, I'm the type of person who doesn't care for constant change. I've stayed in relationships, jobs, and even my old church too long. The Lord would be trying so desperately to do a new thing in my life, but the fear of the unknown would always hold me back. It seems like I always had to take the hard road first and make a complete mess of my life before I would come to my senses and realize that I should have listened to the Lord in the first place.

I came to a place in my life where I got so tired of being out of the will of God that I was willing to take the leap of faith and do what God wanted me to do. To be completely honest with you, He told me to write this book several years ago. I kept procrastinating because I can't stand to write. I don't even send Christmas cards. I thought, *Oh no, Lord . . . anything but write. I hated English class.* I knew I had to obey my Father in heaven because He knows what's best for me. I often wonder what my life would have been like if I would have obeyed a long time ago.

Make Your Dreams a Reality

Haven't you been held down long enough? God wants to do something new in you. He has kept you all of these years throughout your infirmity because He has something greater for you. People might have abused and misused you. Perhaps everyone you trusted turned on you and broke your heart. Maybe some people even tried to convince you that you're not smart enough or that you don't come from the right upbringing. These people are dream killers. They are toxic poison. Don't listen to them; instead, surround yourself with some dream builders.

Go for your dreams! There truly is a champion hidden within you.

Prayer

Dear heavenly Father, I thank You for the awesome plans and purpose You have for my life. I pray that You help me to always go in the direction You've mapped out for my life. Help me to not look to the left or to the right but instead to walk the straight path You have chosen for me. I pray that I never grow impatient while waiting for Your perfect timing. Please mold me into the person You created me to be. And please continue to prepare me for my destiny. May I always be a blessing to others.

Wisdom Words

God created the earth and everything in it, including you and me, so you must believe He can make your dreams a reality. God is always moving on your behalf in the spiritual realm. Just keep calling those things that aren't as if they are. Start thanking God right now before you ever see your dreams come to pass. You will be amazed at the life-changing impact that positive affirmations can have on your attitude and your life.

Begin to say and believe the following statements:

- I can have what God says I can have. I can do what God says I can do, and I can be all that God created me to be.
- I'm more than a conqueror through Christ Jesus.
- God is no respecter of persons; what He did for someone else, He can do for me.
- Greater is He who is in me than he who is in the world. If God is for me, who can be against me?

- I'm the head and not the tail.
- No weapon formed against me shall prosper.
- I'm so blessed that I'm a blessing to others.
- I live in the land of more than enough, not the land of not enough or barely enough.
- I have the mind of Christ.
- I'm so blessed that the blessing of God overtakes me.
- I walk in the favor and wisdom of God all the days of my life.
- One day of favor is worth more than a lifetime of labor.
- The Word I memorize is the Word I'll utilize. The Word was what Jesus used in battle with Satan.
- . When Satan reminds you of your past, you remind him of his future.
- Memorize God's Word to verbalize so you can evangelize.
- Speak the Word of God over every situation that you're wanting God to help you with.
- Don't be afraid to speak the name of Jesus; an opportunity missed is a blessing missed.
- You can be pitiful or powerful; you choose.
- Get rid of stinking thinking and get a checkup from the neck up.
- Quit trying to fit into a world that God is trying to take you out of.
- Your test brings forth your testimony.

- All that you're going through is just positioning you for what God is raising you up for.
- Jesus has set you free, and whomever the Son sets free is free indeed.
- What's ahead of you is so much better than what's behind you.
- Get an attitude of gratitude.
- All things are possible to those who believe.
- Don't get bitter about your past. God wants to use it to walk you into your future.
- Tough times don't last, but tough people do.